Contents

Who were the Romans?.................................4

Invasion.. 6

Revolt and settlement....................... 8

Roman towns.................................10

Home life.....................................12

Family life....................................14

Roman villas.................................16

The Roman army............................ 18

Roads and walls............................ 20

Romans at work............................ 22

Entertainment............................... 24

The Romans and us........................ 26

How do we know?........................... 28

Timeline...................................... 29

Glossary 30

Find out more................................31

Index.. 32

Some words are shown in **bold**, like this. You can find out what they mean by looking in the glossary.

Who were the Romans?

What do you know about the Romans? They won battles, built roads, took baths, and liked bloodthirsty games. But they also did a lot of other things, many of them in Britain. There were Romans here for 500 years. You can still see parts of what they left behind. Even the word "Britain" comes from the Roman word "Britannia".

The Romans came from Italy. Their greatest city was Rome, and they spread across Europe into Africa and western Asia. They were good soldiers, and by winning battles against their neighbours and enemies, they made an **empire**.

▼ Sometimes people re-enact Roman life, for example by dressing as Roman soldiers. This helps us learn what it was like to be a Roman.

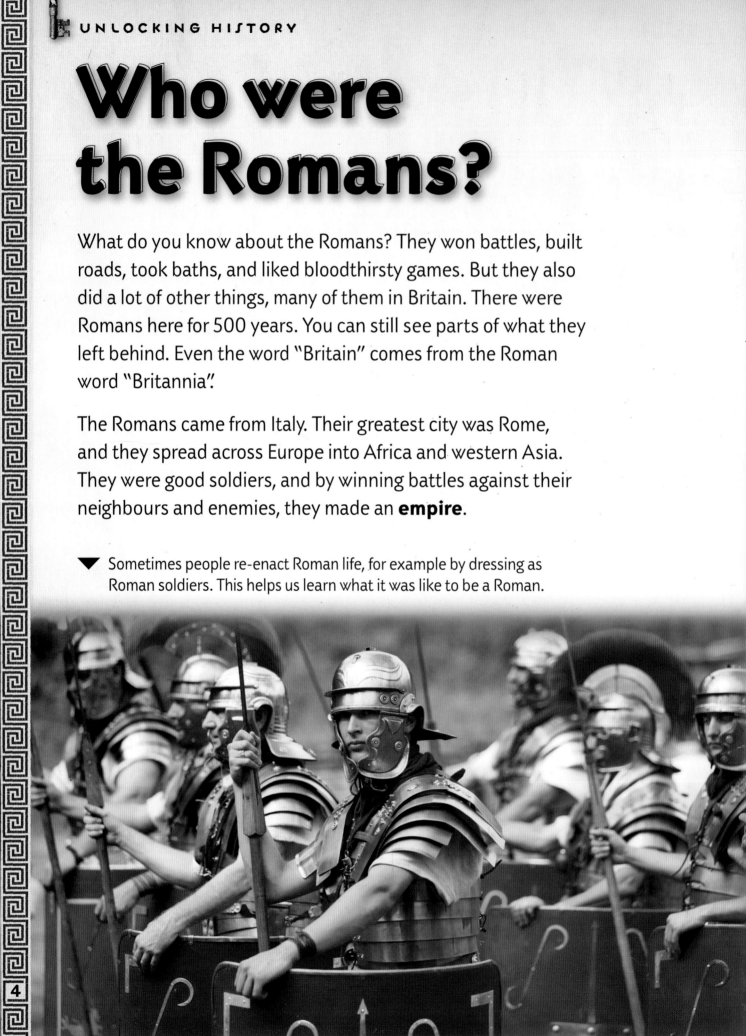

Life in Roman Britain

Brian Williams

www.raintreepublishers.co.uk
Visit our website to find out more information about Raintree books.

To order:
☎ Phone 0845 6044371
🖹 Fax +44 (0) 1865 312263
🖾 Email myorders@raintreepublishers.co.uk

Customers from outside the UK please telephone +44 1865 312262

Raintree is an imprint of Capstone Global Library Limited, a company incorporated in England and Wales having its registered office at 7 Pilgrim Street, London, EC4V 6LB - Registered company number: 6695582

Text © Capstone Global Library Limited 2010
First published in hardback in 2010
First published in paperback in 2011
The moral rights of the proprietor have been asserted.

Edited by Kate de Villiers and Laura Knowles
Designed by Steve Mead and Debbie Oatley
Original illustrations © Capstone Global Library Limited 2010
Illustrated by James Field (pp. 8 and 19) and Calow2Craddock Limited (p. 17)
Picture research by Mica Brancic and Elaine Willis
Production by Alison Parsons
Originated by Chroma Graphics (Overseas) Pte. Ltd
Printed and bound in China by Leo Paper Products Ltd

ISBN 978 0 431 19363 2 (hardback)
14 13 12 11 10
10 9 8 7 6 5 4 3 2 1

ISBN 978 1 406 27496 7 (paperback)
15 14 13
10 9 8 7 6 5 4

British Library Cataloguing in Publication Data
Williams, Brian, 1943-
Life in Roman Britain. -- (Unlocking history)

A full catalogue record for this book is available from the British Library.

Acknowledgements
We would like to thank the following for permission to reproduce photographs: © 2005 TopFoto p. **6** (Woodmansterne); akg-images pp. **23** (Erich Lessing), **21** (Peter Connolly); Alamy pp. **4** (© Nick Turner), **13** (© Linda Kennedy), **20** (Horizon International Images Limited); Ancient Art & Architecture Collection p. **14**; Corbis pp. **7** (© Araldo de Luca), **18** (© Patrick Ward); Norwich Castle Museum and Art Gallery p. **9**; PhotoLibrary p. **27** (Imagestate RM/English Heritage); The Bridgeman Art Library pp. **11** (Museo della Civilta Romana, Rome, Italy), **22** (Verulamium Museum, St.Albans, Hertfordshire, UK), **24** (Verulamium Museum, St.Albans, Hertfordshire, UK); The Trustees of the British Museum p. **28**; TopFoto p. **19**; Topham Picturepoint p. **15**.

Cover photograph of a roundel from a Roman Villa, St Mary, Dorset, 4th century AD reproduced with permission of © 2008 Photolibrary.com (Imagestate RM/Artmedia).

We would like to thank Bill Marriott for his invaluable help in the preparation of this book.

Every effort has been made to contact copyright holders of material reproduced in this book. Any omissions will be rectified in subsequent printings if notice is given to the publishers.

On the western edge of the Roman Empire was Britannia, Roman Britain, though the Romans never conquered the entire island. The people who lived here before the Romans were **Celts**. There were many **tribes**, each with kings or queens.

Most people under Roman rule copied Roman ways. Some learned to read and write in **Latin**, the Romans' language. They took baths like Romans and wore Roman clothes.

This book shows how different kinds of **evidence** – from **archaeology**, writings, and letters – help us to unlock history.

Timeline of the Roman Empire

753 BC	The first city of Rome was built by Romulus and Remus, according to Roman stories
55–54 BC	Roman general Julius Caesar lands twice in Britain. His armies fight the British, but then they leave.
27 BC	Augustus becomes the first Roman emperor
AD **43**	Romans invade Britain and make it part of their empire
AD **60–61**	Boudicca fights the Romans (see page 9)
AD **122**	Romans start to build Hadrian's Wall
AD **364**	Roman Empire is split into West, led by the city of Rome, and East, led by the city of Constantinople
AD **410**	Roman army leaves Britain
AD **476**	Roman Empire in the West ends

BC and AD

We use BC to show dates before the **Christian** religion began. We count BC dates backwards (so 55 BC is the year before 54 BC). AD shows a date is after the Christian religion began. We count AD dates forwards (so AD 44 is the year after AD 43).

Invasion

Before the Romans came to Britain, people in the south of the country could make a short trip across the sea to Gaul, which was part of Rome's **empire**. Gaul covered a large part of Western Europe, including modern France, Belgium, and southern Germany. The Roman general, Julius Caesar, came to Britain twice, fought the British **tribes**, and then sailed back to Gaul. The Romans were surprised to see British **Celts** dash into battle in **chariots** pulled by horses. Romans drove chariots mainly for fun.

▼ This is Maiden Castle, a hill fort in Dorset. The Roman army attacked it.

For more than 80 years after Julius Caesar left, the Romans left Britain alone. Romans and Britons met in Gaul, and got to know one another through **trade**. The Romans liked British wheat, gold, dogs, and warm winter coats! The Britons – rich ones anyway – liked Roman wine, pottery, and coins.

In AD 43, the Romans invaded Britain. An army of 40,000 soldiers landed from ships, and marched inland to attack the British **hill forts**. The Romans soon took over southern Britain, though a brave warrior-leader called Caratacus kept fighting until he was captured and taken to Rome.

This is a bust (model head) of the general Julius Caesar.

Julius Caesar

Julius Caesar (100–44 BC) wrote about how the British in chariots tried to outwit Roman cavalry (horsemen): they "fell back on purpose … then jumped down and fought on foot". Caesar was Rome's most famous general. In 44 BC, Caesar was stabbed to death in Rome. This was 10 years after his second visit to Britain.

How do we know?

The British Celts did not write about the Roman wars. What we know comes from Roman writers, such as Julius Caesar (who saw Britain for himself) and Tacitus (someone who wrote down what others told him). Tacitus tells us that Caratacus was impressed when he saw Rome. "Why, when you have all this, do you envy us our poor huts?" he asked.

Revolt and settlement

Some British people liked Roman rule. Others did not like paying **taxes** to Rome, and protested at Roman laws stopping them carrying spears and swords. The Iceni **tribe** of East Anglia rose in **revolt** against the Romans. Their leader was Queen Boudicca (see page 9). Other tribes joined in, and Boudicca's army burned the Roman cities of Colchester, London, and St Albans. We know about this from **archaeology**, and from what the Romans wrote.

Roman army

- ☑ cavalry
- ☑ swords, daggers, and spears
- ☑ shields
- ☑ helmets and armour
- ☑ forts
- ☑ one empire
- ☑ bravery
- ☑ ships
- ☑ roads
- ☑ organization
- ☑ siege machines
- ☑ discipline and training

Celtic Warriors

- ☑ chariots
- ☑ swords, daggers, and spears
- ☑ shields
- ☑ some helmets and armour
- ☑ forts
- ☑ lots of tribes
- ☑ bravery

A checklist helps to compare the Romans and Celts as fighters.

However, the Romans were not beaten. Roman soldiers marched along new Roman roads from Wales and the north of England, and fought Boudicca's much bigger army. The Romans' victory made sure that Britain stayed part of the Roman **Empire**. By around AD 80 the Romans had gone as far north as Scotland. They fought the tribes there, but did not conquer them. Instead, they built Hadrian's Wall to defend the northern **frontier** of Roman Britain, and another wall, the Antonine Wall, in Scotland.

After the revolt, the Romans treated the British more fairly. The British came to like many Roman ways. They settled down to life as part of the Roman Empire.

▼ These Iceni coins were buried in about AD 61, the year Boudicca led her revolt. Who might have hidden them?

Boudicca
Boudicca was born around 30 BC. When she was 18 she married King Prasutagus of the Iceni tribe, in what is now Norfolk. They had two daughters. Prasutagus died in around AD 59, and Boudicca became Queen of the Iceni. After she and her family were badly treated by the Romans, she led a revolt. After her army was defeated, it is believed that Boudicca killed herself.

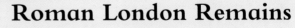

Roman London Remains
Beneath the streets of modern London, archaeologists have found an ash-black layer of clay – the remains of Roman houses burned by Boudicca's army.

Roman towns

The **Celts** were farmers, and lived in villages of wood and mud houses. For defence against enemies, they built **hill forts**. You can walk around some of them today, though only grassy banks and ditches remain. Some forts were very big, with high wooden walls and steep ditches. Inside, the king and his people felt safe from attack.

Though many Romans were also farmers, Romans liked town life. They built towns everywhere they went. Their streets were neat, built in a criss-cross pattern. There were stone walls with gates for people to go in and out. There were town halls, law courts, piped water and drains, public baths with hot and cold pools, theatres, and stadiums.

Towns were important for **trade**. Shops opened onto the street, and the shopkeeper's family lived in rooms at the back. Shops sold oil for lighting and cooking, food, shoes, tools, furniture, clay pots, and all the other things people needed. The Romans used coins, like we do, but not paper money. Traders from all over the Roman **Empire** came by road and river to sell luxury goods, such as wine, pottery, and glassware. Roman London was a busy port. With about 50,000 people living there, it was easily the biggest city in Roman Britain.

New town, old name

Big Celtic villages became Roman towns. For example, the Roman name for Silchester in Hampshire was "Calleva Atrebatum". This is **Latin** for "town in the wood of the Atrebates". The Atrebates were a Celtic **tribe**.

Place names can give clues about the history of a country.

Roman Britain's biggest towns

This table compares how many people lived in Roman towns, and how many people live in those towns today.

Town/city (Roman name)	Estimated Roman population	Population today
London (Londinium)	50,000	7.5 million
Colchester (Camulodunum)	15,000	100,000
St Albans (Verulamium)	15,000	64,000
Cirencester (Corinium)	10,000	18,000
York (Eboracum)	8,000	137,000

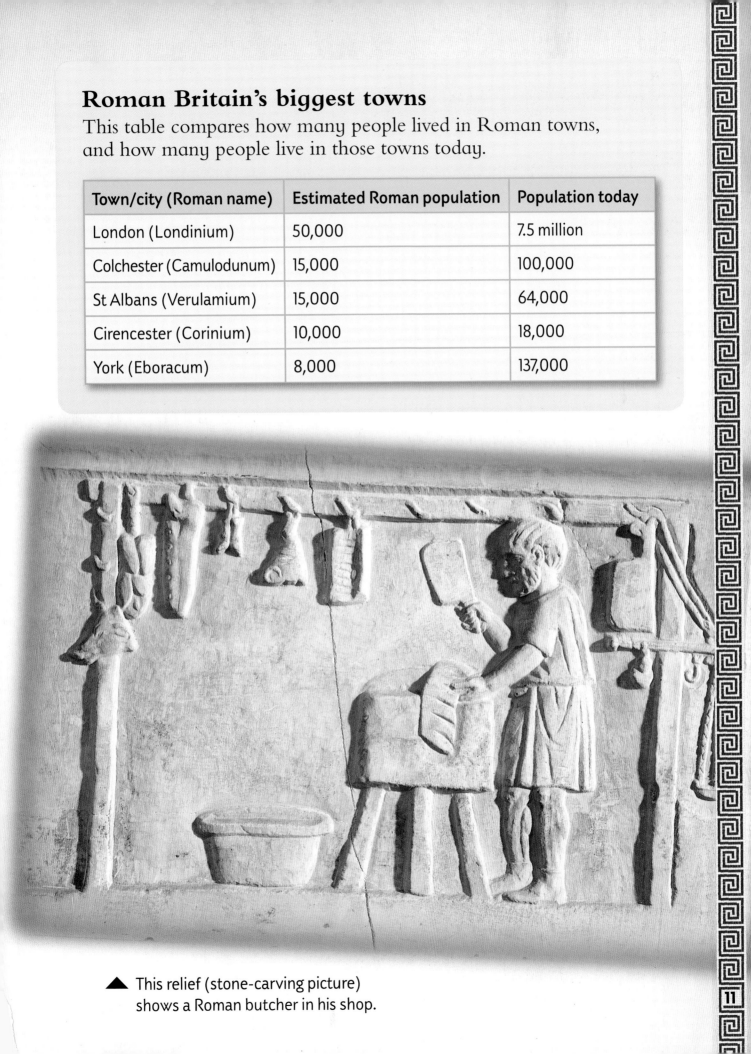

▲ This relief (stone-carving picture) shows a Roman butcher in his shop.

Home life

The **Celts** lived in wooden huts. Rich Romans had fine town houses built of stone, or large country houses they called villas. Poor people lived in small huts, or in rooms in a building, for which a family paid money (rent) to the building's owner. Many of the poorest people were **slaves**, who slept in their owners' house, or in an outbuilding.

In a Roman house there was not much furniture, just wooden stools and couches, with a "best" chair kept for old people and visitors. People slept in wooden beds on mattresses stuffed with straw or wool, snug beneath furs or wool blankets. A rich person's house had floors covered with small coloured tiles or stones, arranged to make pictures called mosaics. There were paintings on the plaster walls, too. A poor house had dirt floors, with only a mat of woven reeds or a sheepskin rug.

Slaves prepared food in the kitchen on a stone table and cooked the food on a fire. Slaves also carried wood to burn in the Roman central heating system, known as the hypocaust. This sent hot air under floors and up inside hollow walls, to warm the rooms.

Warmth and light

In a Roman house, people kept warm by burning charcoal or wood in iron baskets called braziers. At night, people lit oil lamps. They also burned candles made from wax or animal fat.

▲ The underfloor remains of this hypocaust are at Bignor Roman Villa in West Sussex.

Rich Romans ate well, and a new table dish was rabbit. The 2,000-year-old bones of a rabbit, found in Norfolk in 2005, suggest that it was the Romans who first brought rabbits to Britain. With no sugar, people sweetened fruit, cakes, and pastries with honey. From **archaeological** finds at army forts, we know soldiers ate healthy whole-grain bread with poppy seeds. Poor people got by on bowls of porridge and thick vegetable soup.

Roman food often tasted fishy. Their favourite sauce was made from fish, and they added it to all sorts of dishes.

13

Family life

Rich Roman families had strict rules, made by the father. He was often away at work all day, so his wife and children did not see him much. The mother ran the home. Boys, and some girls, went to school, or had lessons at home from a private teacher. Poor children were lucky if they learned to read and write.

Religion was important to Romans. At home, a Roman family kept small statues of gods and household "spirits" to bring good luck. Romans in Britain "borrowed" local British gods to add to their own, and by about 400, many were **Christians**.

Girls, rich or poor, often had a harder time than boys. Most were married by the age of 14, and had to work hard. Before her wedding, a girl gave away her toys to show she had grown up. No woman ever ruled Rome, but British **Celts** had women leaders, such as Boudicca. Roman women in Britain probably had more say in family affairs.

Toys and games
Children's playthings included:
- Dolls, toy swords, balls, miniature clay figures
- Marbles (pebbles or nuts)
- Board games with counters and dice
- Pet cats, dogs, caged birds, and tortoises.

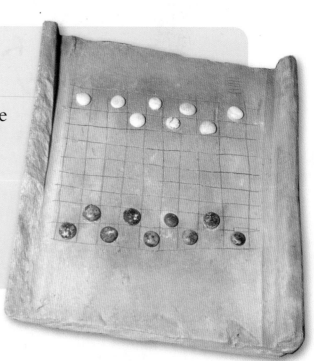

This is a Roman board game with playing pieces, or counters. ▶

A rich family owned **slaves** to do the hard work. Slaves were given occasional holidays, however. They might go on a family outing to the "games" at the town's amphitheatre (large circular stadium) to cheer **chariot** races, and boo and hiss at **gladiator** fights (see page 24).

◄ This pottery beaker was found at Colchester. It was made in around AD 175.

What can we tell from this beaker? Experts can read the men's names, scratched in the clay of the beaker. The man with the shield was called Memno. The other man's name was Valentinus. The beaker also shows that Valentinus only wore his armour on one arm and that Memno was left-handed.

Roman villas

A villa was a rich family's country house, with a farm. Not all villas were big houses, but most were built near a road, for carts to come and go. The main house had rooms arranged around a courtyard garden. From Roman books, paintings, and from finds made by **archaeologists**, we know that Roman gardeners liked hedges in patterns, apple and pear trees, grape vines, rose bushes, and herbs. We know Romans used herbs in cooking and for medicines.

The villa-farm was often run by a manager or "overseer". The manager gave orders to the workers, many of whom were **slaves**. There were lots of jobs to do. The farm produced food for the local town and army camp.

Jobs on a villa-farm

- Cooking
- Cleaning
- Making pottery
- Growing vegetables and fruit
- Cutting firewood
- Spinning wool from sheep and goats
- Weaving cloth
- Making iron tools
- Making wooden furniture
- Driving carts
- Making baskets from rushes
- Grinding grain to make flour
- Making plant dyes to colour cloth
- Digging ditches

We know about some villas in Roman Britain from what archaeologists have found. Sometimes the hidden ruins of a long-lost building are seen from the air. Sometimes the buried stone walls and floors of a villa are found when builders are clearing a site for a road or new homes. From these finds, we can picture what a villa was like.

Plant and food remains, such as seeds or meat bones, show what people grew or ate.

▲ A Roman villa. Modern pictures of villas are made using **evidence** from archaeology and from Roman descriptions and paintings. See the courtyard garden with its shaped hedges, road, and surrounding farm land.

The Roman army

Many clues to what life was like in Roman Britain, such as walls, forts, weapons, tombstones, and food remains, come from places where the Roman army was based. The army kept the peace in Roman Britain. Soldiers also built forts and roads. The key battle force in the army was the **legion**. Each legion had about 5,000 soldiers, and had a name and number, such as 2nd Augusta (named after Emperor Augustus).

The three main Roman army bases in Britain were at Chester and York in England, and Caerleon in Wales. Soldiers also lived at many other places, such as Colchester and Hadrian's Wall.

▼ Hadrian's Wall was built by Roman soldiers.

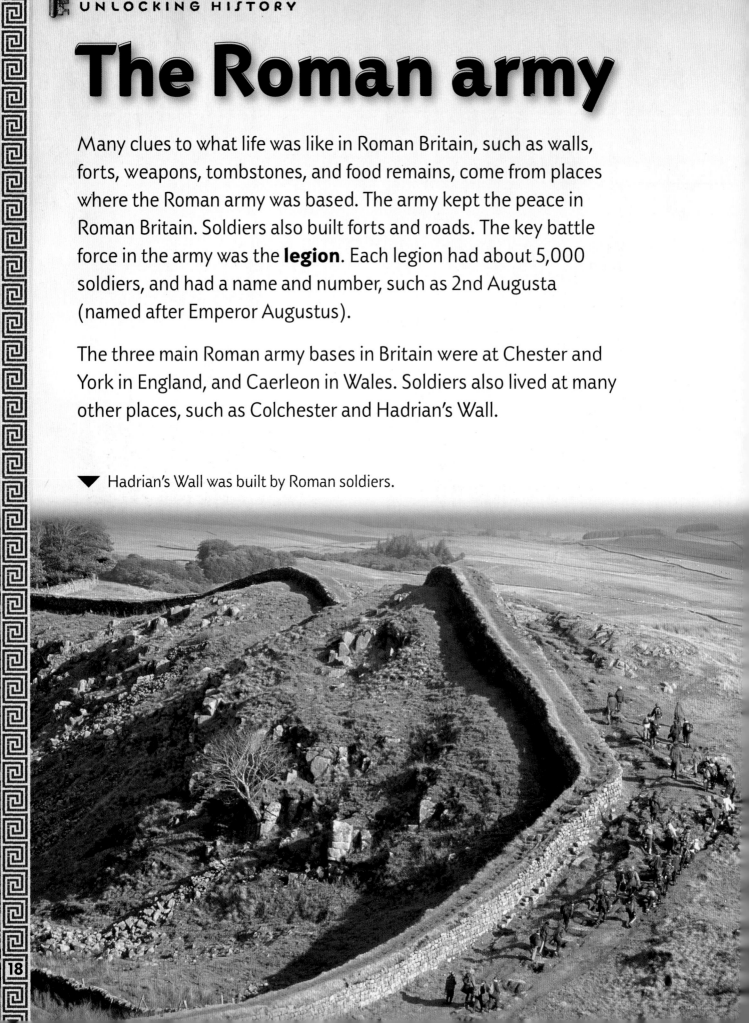

Roman soldiers practised fighting with wooden swords. These were heavier than real swords, so battle-fighting seemed easier. Soldiers could swim rivers, build forts and bridges, and dig ditches. They could ride horses, throw spears, and, if attacked, take shelter behind their shields. The army had infantry (foot-soldiers) and cavalry (horsemen). To bash down walls and scatter enemy troops, the Roman soldiers fired catapults and giant crossbows!

Finds made by **archaeologists** at Roman army bases tell us about the soldiers' lives. For example, the Colchester tombstone of Longinus Sdapeze tells us that he was a cavalry soldier from Bulgaria. He probably came to Colchester with one of the four legions that invaded Britain in AD 43.

metal helmet

kit on pole

chest and shoulder armour of iron and leather

sword

shield

javelin (throwing spear)

boots

▲ This picture shows what a Roman soldier wore and the kit he had to carry.

The tombstone of Longinus Sdapeze, who died between AD 43 and 49.

Roads and walls

Before the Romans came, Britain had very few roads, just ancient tracks walked by people for a thousand years or more. Roman soldiers built new roads, so they could march to fight an enemy. The roads made it easier for people to travel for **trade** or visits. Roman roads were built to last.

▼ Some Roman roads can still be seen. Some modern roads even follow routes planned by Roman engineers across Britain.

Roman road building

Can you put these stages in Roman road building in the right order?
1. Get soldiers to tramp along the road in their heavy nailed sandals
2. Lay cement and flat stones to make a smooth surface
3. Clear the way, chop down trees, fill in holes
4. Survey the route. Make it as straight as possible (unless uphill, then zig-zag)
5. Lay a base of clay, chalk, or gravel – or timber if ground is boggy

Answer: 4, 3, 5, 2, 1

When travelling, most people walked. Rich men rode horses. Rich ladies sat in carriages. Farmers drove heavy carts pulled by oxen (a type of cattle). Traders led pack horses with bags or bundles tied on their backs. People also used boats to move heavy loads of wheat, timber, or jars of wine.

As well as roads, Romans built walls around towns and forts, and across country. Their most famous wall is Hadrian's Wall (see page 18), built to mark the **frontier** between Roman Britain and the non-Roman North (Scotland). It took eight years to build the 118-kilometre (73-mile) wall. Some of the soldiers guarding the wall came from sunny southern Europe – the Roman army had men from all over the **empire**. In cold British winters, shivering soldiers wrote letters home asking families to send warm clothes!

▲ This picture shows what the roman toilets at Hadrian's Wall would have looked like.

Fun fact

Archaeologists have found army toilets at Hadrian's Wall. The toilets had wooden seats with holes. Instead of toilet paper, Romans used sponges or moss on sticks, which they washed in water piped in from streams and stone tanks filled with rainwater.

Romans at work

Work in Roman times often meant a lot of backache! The Romans had few machines. Most people worked with their hands, and many jobs needed strong muscles and expert fingers. Some Roman tools have survived, and are now in museums. We can also look at Roman pictures and carvings of people going about their daily tasks.

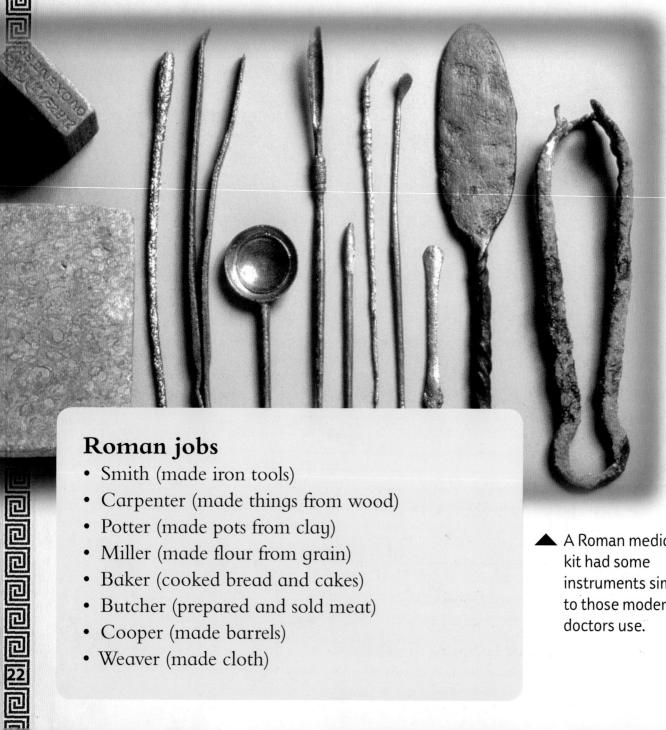

▲ A Roman medical kit had some instruments similar to those modern doctors use.

Roman jobs

- Smith (made iron tools)
- Carpenter (made things from wood)
- Potter (made pots from clay)
- Miller (made flour from grain)
- Baker (cooked bread and cakes)
- Butcher (prepared and sold meat)
- Cooper (made barrels)
- Weaver (made cloth)

Slaves did the dirty jobs. They swept the streets, dug ditches, and collected waste from toilets, which was then used to put goodness back into the soil on farm fields. Slaves also worked as servants in the homes of rich people. Slaves were fed by their owners, but not paid. If they were beaten and ran away, they were chased – and beaten even more!

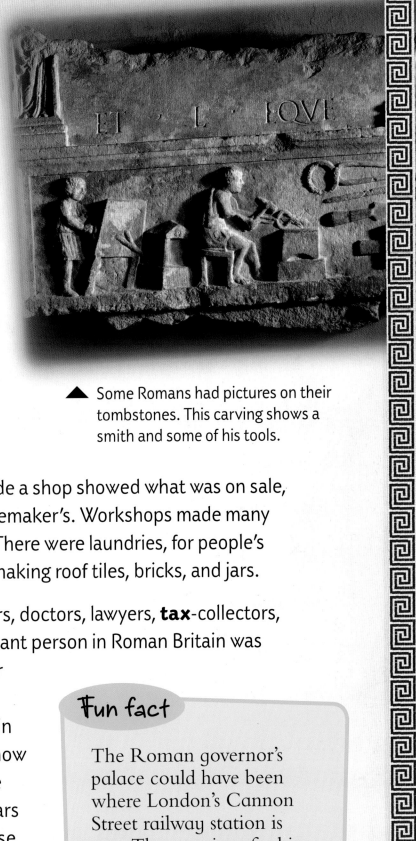

▲ Some Romans had pictures on their tombstones. This carving shows a smith and some of his tools.

In a Roman town, a sign outside a shop showed what was on sale, for example a sandal for a shoemaker's. Workshops made many of the things people needed. There were laundries, for people's washing, and small factories making roof tiles, bricks, and jars.

The top jobs were army officers, doctors, lawyers, **tax**-collectors, and **priests**. The most important person in Roman Britain was the governor. He was the ruler and lived in a splendid palace in London. Only the emperor in Rome had more power. We know the names and dates of all the governors for the first 200 years or so of Roman Britain, because the Romans kept a list. The first governor was Aulus Plautius. He was in charge from AD 43 (the year of the invasion) until AD 47.

Fun fact

The Roman governor's palace could have been where London's Cannon Street railway station is now. The remains of a big Roman building have been found there.

Entertainment

Celts enjoyed storytelling, singing, hunting animals, and horse-racing. People in Roman Britain went on enjoying these things, but also had new Roman pleasures. Men and women went to the public baths to bathe, relax, and gossip. Rich young men kept fit by swimming, running, horse-riding, or wrestling. Most large towns had a stadium, with seats for the crowd around the arena (playing area). Rich and poor all crowded in to watch the "games". The games were very bloody, because killing was part of the fun. Crowds cheered fights to the death between **gladiators**, and laughed as lions or bulls chased helpless prisoners.

▼ The theatre at Verulanium (St Albans) probably looked like this modern artist's reconstruction.

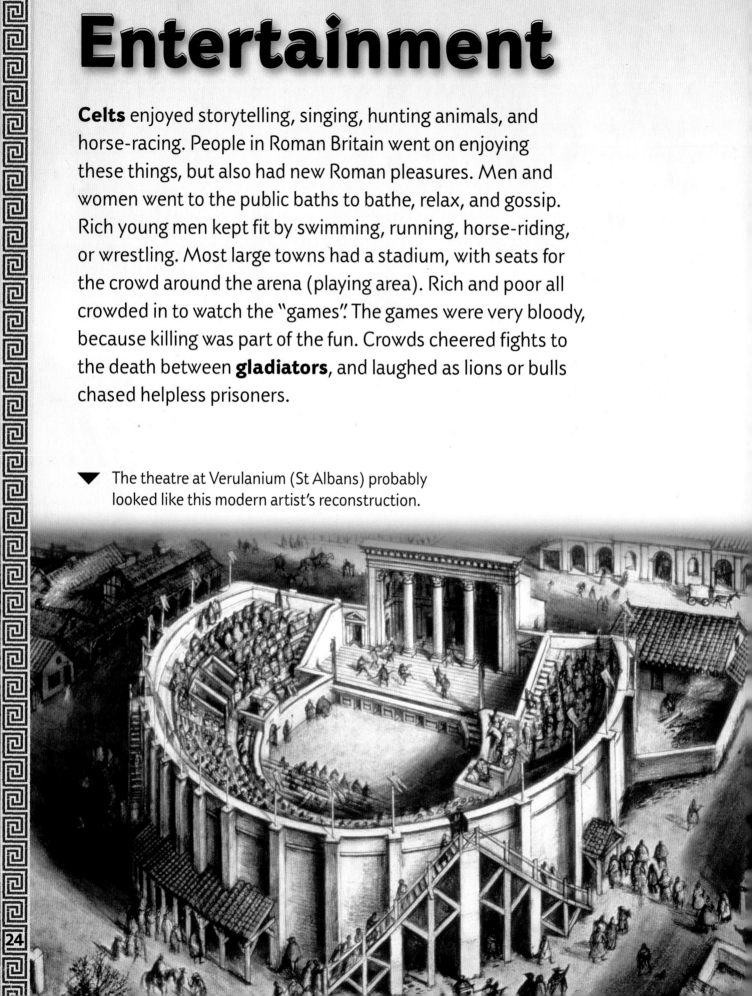

Chariot racing was exciting, with lots of crashes. A chariot was a small two-wheeled cart, with a driver, and usually four horses. The chariots raced several times around an oval track. Chariot racing was popular because British Celts loved horses, and had driven war chariots into battles against the Romans!

What do you think?
Why do you think Roman rulers put on fights and violent games?
• They needed money from selling tickets
• They thought the games would amuse the Roman gods
• Giving them entertainment stopped poor people grumbling
• Football had not been invented
• Roman rulers liked to fight, to show off
• Romans were cruel and violent much of the time

At home, rich people gave parties, with poetry readings, music, and dancing. At the theatre, people liked funny plays, with comic actors wearing masks. The Romans loved gardens, and they brought to Britain about 400 different types of new plants, including roses, parsley, and walnut trees.

Fun fact

A Roman dinner
We can read Roman recipes in Roman cookery books. A dinner party for rich people might start with eggs, oysters, fish, and snails, followed by wild boar, venison (deer), hare, dormice, and a stuffed peacock. Romans ate dinner quite early, at about 4 p.m. Poor people did not have such rich foods – they ate a lot of porridge, with vegetables.

The Romans and us

Roman Britain ended in the AD 400s, when the Roman army left to defend Rome. New settlers moved in from Europe. These were the Anglo-Saxons. They gave southern Britain a new name – England, meaning "land of the Angles".

Roman towns were no longer busy, well-run centres of **trade** and government. People moved away, and many became farmers once more. For hundreds of years, no towns were as wealthy as the Roman towns had been. Yet much of Roman Britain remained.

Roman roads went on being used by travellers for hundreds of years. The Romans gave Britain its first real palace – Fishbourne, near Chichester. Roman forts, such as Pevensey in East Sussex, were taken over and added to by later peoples, such as the Normans. Many modern cities, such as London and York, stand on Roman remains, some of which can still be glimpsed among the newer buildings.

Rome also changed the way people thought about government, law, religion, science, art, and literature. Many English words come from **Latin**. Video, for example, comes from the Latin word *videre*, meaning "to see".

Roman Numerals

You will sometimes see Roman numerals, in dates or on clocks. XI on a clock means 11. IX means 9. Can you tell what LXVII is in the numbers we use today?
Clue: I = 1, V = 5, X = 10, L = 50, C = 100, D = 500, M = 1,000

Answer: 67

England's population

A country's population (the number of people it has) does not always rise. It was 1,000 years before England's population was again as big as in Roman times. The Romans brought peace and there was enough food to feed over 4 million people. Later, wars, famine, and disease (the Black Death of 1348, for instance) reduced the population.

Date	Population
Roman Britain	4–6 million
England in 1086	about 2 million
England in 1300	about 4 million
England in 1540	about 3.5 million

▼ This Roman lighthouse at Dover (left) was later used as a bell tower for the Saxon church built next to it (right).

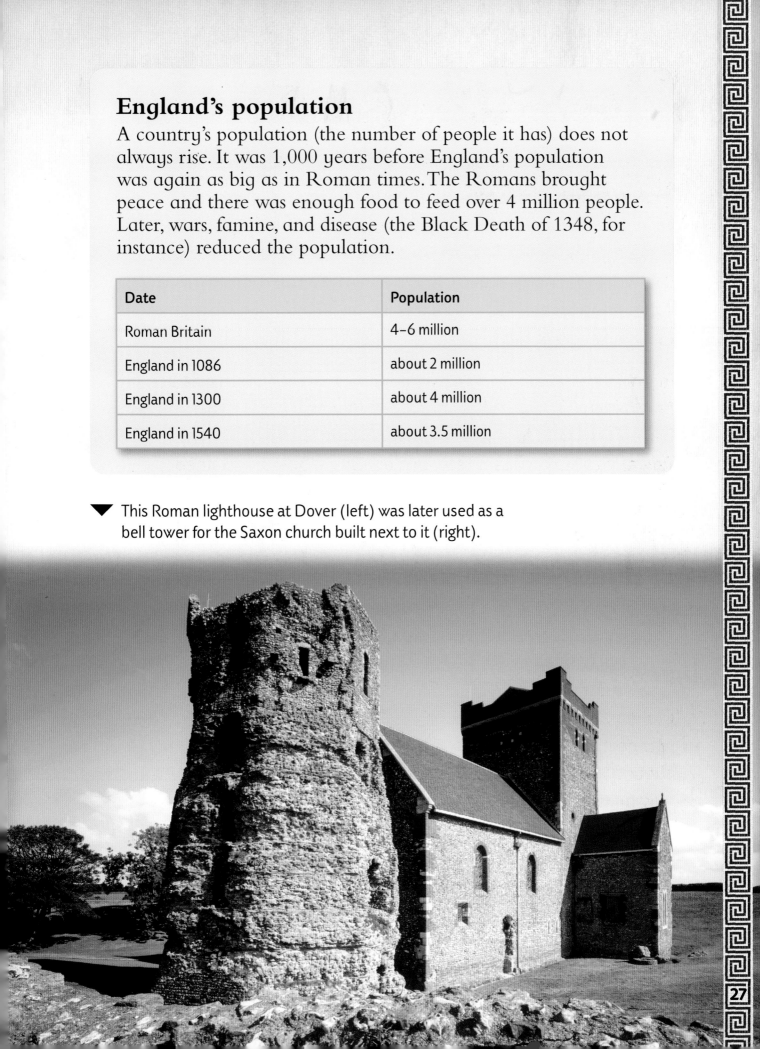

How do we know?

We can find out some information about Roman life from letters found by archaeologists. The Vindolanda Tablets are a collection of Roman letters, found at a Roman fort (Vindolanda, in Northumberland). The letters were written on tablets of thin wood, with pen and ink, and thrown away on rubbish tips between AD 80 and 130. One letter is a birthday invitation from Claudia Severa to her friend Sulpicia Lepidina. She wrote:

"On 11th September, sister, for the day of the celebration of my birthday, I give you a warm invitation to make sure that you come to us, to make the day more enjoyable for me ..."

▼ Claudia Severa's letter, written with ink on wood.

Roman letters are rare finds. The Vindolanda Tablets are now safe in the British Museum, London.

The **Celts** who lived in Britain before the Romans came did not write books about themselves. We know about them from what is left, such as the **hill fort** at Maiden Castle in Dorset, or things **archaeologists** find, such as a rusty sword or a coin. The Romans left a lot more **evidence** in buildings, art, and books. We can read writings by famous people, such as Julius Caesar, and by ordinary people, such as Claudia Severa. We can visit the ruins of Roman walls and buildings. There is a wealth of evidence to help unlock the history of life in Roman Britain.

Timeline

BC

753 According to stories, Rome was built by Romulus and Remus

500 By this time, **Celts** are living in Britain in **tribes**

55 Romans, led by Julius Caesar, land in Britain for the first time

54 Caesar returns to Britain, fights the Celts, and then leaves

44 Caesar is murdered in Rome

AD

41 Claudius becomes emperor of Rome; Cunobelinus, king of the Catuvellauni tribe, dies

43 Claudius orders an invasion of Britain

51 Caratacus is defeated by the Romans in battle

61 Boudicca, Queen of the Iceni, leads a **revolt** against Roman rule

79 The Roman general, Agricola, invades Caledonia (Scotland)

84 Romans defeat Scottish tribes at the battle of Mons Graupius

90 The Vindolanda fort in Northumberland is built

110 The Roman **Empire** reaches its greatest size

122 The Roman army begins building Hadrian's Wall in north Britain

142 Romans build the Antonine Wall in Scotland

337 Emperor Constantine, who made **Christianity** the religion of the Roman Empire, dies

364 The Roman Empire is split into two – the Western Empire, led by the city of Rome, and the Eastern Empire, led by the city of Constantinople

400 By this time, Christianity is the main religion of Britain

410 The last Roman soldiers leave Britain

476 The Roman Empire in the West ends

Glossary

archaeologist expert in archaeology, the study of the past from evidence often found beneath the soil or under the sea

Celt people who lived in Britain and other parts of Europe and who fought the Romans

chariot two-wheeled cart drawn by horses

Christian follower of the religion first taught by Jesus Christ

empire large area with many peoples living under the rule of an emperor

evidence picture, writing, an object, or someone's account, which tells how things were at a particular time

frontier boundary between Roman-ruled territory and another

hill fort Celtic stronghold, on top of a hill, defended by fences, earth banks, and ditches

gladiator trained fighter, who fought and died in the Roman arena

Latin language spoken by the Romans

legion unit of the Roman army, usually with around 5,000 "legionaries"

priest person in charge of religious practices. In Roman times priests looked after temples.

revolt uprising or rebellion against a ruler

slave servant who was not free, and who belonged to a master

taxes money or other payment made by people to the government

trade buying and selling goods

tribe group of people sharing a similar way of life and beliefs

Find out more

Books

Usborne History of Roman Britain, Ruth Brocklehurst
(Usborne Publishing Ltd, 2008)

Staying Alive in Ancient Rome, Brenda Williams and Brian Williams
(Raintree, 2007)

Voyages Through Time: Ancient Rome, Peter Ackroyd
(Dorling Kindersley Publishers Ltd, 2005)

Websites

This site gives lots of information and facts about the Romans,
with activities: www.bbc.co.uk/schools/romans

Find out more about different Roman topics such as Hadrian's Wall:
http://www.britainexpress.com/History/Roman_Britain_index.htm

Places to visit

These are just some of the places you could visit to discover more
about Roman Britain:

Bath – Roman baths

Caerleon, Gwent, Wales – Roman fort

Cirencester, Gloucestershire – amphitheatre and museum

Colchester, Essex – Roman military town, and a museum in a Norman
castle on the site of a Roman temple

Fishbourne, West Sussex – remains of a very large villa or palace

Lullingstone, Kent – Roman villa

Maiden Castle, Dorset – Celtic hill fort

Silchester, Hampshire – Roman town defences and amphitheatre

St Albans, Hertfordshire – remains of Roman town, including a theatre

Vindolanda at Chesterholm, Northumberland – fort-settlement on
Hadrian's Wall

Index

Anglo-Saxons **26**
armour and weapons **8, 15, 18, 19**
army **7, 8, 18–19, 21, 26**

Boudicca, Queen **5, 8, 9, 14, 29**

Caesar, Julius **5, 6, 7, 28, 29**
Caratacus **7, 29**
Celts **5, 6, 7, 8, 10, 12, 14, 24, 28, 29**
central heating **12, 13**
chariots **6, 7, 15, 25**
children **14**
Christianity **5, 14, 29**
coins **7, 9, 10**
Colchester **8, 18**

education **14**
entertainment **24–25**

family life **14-15**
farming **16, 23, 26**
food **12, 13, 16, 25**
frontiers **9, 21**
furniture **12**

gardens **16, 25**
Gaul **6, 7**
gladiators **15, 24**
governors **23**

Hadrian's Wall **5, 9, 18, 21, 29**
hill forts **6, 7, 10, 28**
home life **12–13, 16–17**

Iceni **8, 9**
invasion of Britain **5, 7, 29**

Latin **5, 10, 26**
legions **18**
letters **28**
London **8, 9, 10, 23, 26**

marriage **14**
medicine **16, 22**

numerals, Roman **26**

palaces **23, 26**
place names **10**
population **11, 27**
pottery **7, 10, 15, 22**
public baths **10, 24**

religion **5, 14**
rich and poor **7, 12–16, 15, 21, 23, 24, 25**
roads **4, 9, 16–18, 20–21, 26**
Roman Empire **4, 5, 6, 9, 10, 21, 29**

Rome **4, 5, 7–8, 23, 26, 29**

St Albans **8, 24**
Scotland **9, 29**
shops **10, 11, 23**
slaves **12, 15, 16, 23**
soldiers **4, 8, 13, 18-19, 20, 21**

Tacitus **7**
taxes **8, 23**
timelines **5, 29**
toilets **21, 23**
towns **10–11, 26**
toys and games **14**
trade **7, 10**
travel **21**
tribes **5, 6, 8, 9, 10**

villas **13–14, 16–17**
Vindolanda Tablets **28**

warriors, Celtic **8**
women **14**
work **16, 22–23**

York **18, 26**